POEM

AMIR OR

WAXWING BOOKS

Amir Or

Amir Or, poet, translator, and editor, was born in Tel Aviv, Israel in 1956. Or has published seven books of poetry and his poetry collections in translation include: *Poetry is a Criminal Girl* (Arabic, Faradis publishers, Paris 1995), *Miracle* (English\Hebrew, Poetry Ireland, Dublin 1998), *Drowning, He Breaths Living Water* (Macedonian, Peliades series of the SPE poetry festival, 2000) and *Language Says* (English, PM publications, Chattanooga, 2001). His poems have also been anthologized and published in more than 20 languages. Or has taken part in many international literary conferences and festivals, and worked as a guest writer in several cultural institutions, among which are the University of Iowa, the Literarische Colloquium Berlin, and the Jewish and Hebrew Centre at the University of Oxford. His collections of poetry include: *I Look Through The Monkeys' Eyes* (1987), *Faces* (1991), *Ransoming The Dead* (1994), *So!* (1995) *Poem* (1996) and *Day* (1998). His last book *The Song of Tahira* (2001) is a novel written in metered prose.

Or studied philosophy and Comparative Religion at the Hebrew University in Jerusalem, where he later lectured on Ancient Greek Religion. He has published articles on poetry, classical studies and religious studies, and has taught these subjects. He has also published several books of translations, among which are *The Gospel of Thomas* (1992), *Limb-Loosening Desire; An Anthology of Erotic Greek Poetry* (1993), *Stories From The Mahabharata* (1998) and *To a Woman* by Shuntaro Tanikawa (2000, with Akiko Takahashi). For his poetry he has been awarded the Prime Minister's Award, Bernstein Award and Holon Award; and for his translations of poetry from ancient Greek an honorary award from the Minister of Culture.

Since its foundation, Or has been chief editor of the Helicon Society for the Advancement of Poetry in Israel. He has initiated and developed Helicon projects and is editor of its journal, series of poetry books and the"Sha'ar Festival" for new poetry. He is also local coordinator for "Poets for Peace" (the UN sponsored UPC venture).

Amir Or

°

Poem

°

translated from Hebrew by

Helena Berg

°

Translation editor and Afterword: Fiona Sampson

ⓘDEDALUS

Waxwing Books ~ 24 The Heath ~ Cypress Downs ~ Dublin 6W
Ireland
Editor: John F. Deane

o

© Amir Or and Helena Berg 2004
© Afterword Fiona Sampson 2004

published in Hebrew by the Hakibbutz Hameuchad Publishing House Ltd. 1996

o

Waxwing Books are distributed by The Dedalus Press :
represented and distributed in the U.S.A. and Canada by **Dufour Editions Ltd.**, P.O. Box 7, Chester
Springs, Pennsylvania 19425
in the UK by **Central Books**, 99 Wallis Road, London E9 5LN

The Dedalus Press receives financial assistance from
An Chomhairle Ealaíon, The Arts Council, Ireland.
Printed in Dublin by Johnswood Press

For you
I will awake the harp by dawn

Chapters

A seed sown in sand waits years for rain

[1]

This poem will be a poem of another century, not different from ours.
This poem will be safely hidden under heaps of words until,

among the last grains in the hourglass,
like a ship in a bottle, it will be seen. This poem

that will speak of innocence. And ordinary people,
who seem thrown up by the course of events, like late-coming gods,

will listen to it for no reason that wasn't there before,
raising their backs like snakes

out of the junk,   and there won't be anywhere else
to hurry from, and it won't have an end

different from its beginning. It won't be rich
and won't be poor. Won't bother anymore to keep promises

or carry out what it says
and won't understate or puff itself from here to there.

This poem, if it speaks to you, woman, won't call you
muse babe, and won't sleep with you like its fathers did;

or if to you, man, won't kneel or kill, won't apply make-up
and won't take off its words and flesh, as it has not   has not —

what? Maybe now I'll summon it, the bad poem
of the century: here, sick with health it's barely walking

drags its legs in the sticky current of contemporary thought
or gets stopped to show its papers   and have its trivia counted

on an abacus. The inventory: flowers and staples,
corpses (yes, no worry), tall glasses. After staples —

also butterflies and many footprints and other hooks and shelves
for the arguments of scholarly criticism, and also just to fool around, teeth

against teeth, with the chaotic smiles of a chameleon   that doesn't know
its colours long since turned into a parable. Or in incomprehensible tranquillity

to try someone else's luck in games of to and fro
that have no goal other than, let's say,

a bit of fun the length of a line. Spread orange on the blue
of evening sky: now, plaster on a little cloud. Climb

on, look down: sea of sea, sand of sand.
Or fingers. Ten jointed worms

move with inexplicable charm. Now they encircle
a sphere whose curve is faulty, wonderful, fleshy,   furthermore

you can say a word (it's a fruit, it's called
a peach). And these words   their taste is full of the taste

of being, of a tone that accompanies the sight with wonder
and not with a thought-slamming din. And this is the poem:

it sings, let's say, to the tar that stuck to your foot at the beach,
to plastic bottles, to its own words. All it sees

is black on white, transparent or grainy.
It is no less naked than you. Also no more. Only through this exactness

that has no measure except the curves of a bitch's body,
a pot of cyclamen or a hair on a bath rail.

Creatures here don't want to know. Creatures
there, wanting only that, are, for now, the possibility

of becoming creatures here, of becoming this antiquity
that has nothing to say other than *me, me*, without limit

without you. A dog lies on a step in the afternoon
sun and does not distinguish itself from the flies.

Rain. He is torn out from himself.

[2]

You bite, swallow, actually crack line after line
in front of this screen, spit the spaces as if they're

a Hungarian sound track. And it's OK by me, because it's OK
by you: to live between walls, to be covered by them and move

into a foetal rhythm: eat and drink, fill up a petrol tank,
order groceries, read poems, sleep. Faster:

a filmed commercial, video clips,
a microwave, peep booths at a porno movie. Faster:

capsules, transfusion, electrodes. Faster:
don't be born. You are not and you don't have an existence now

outside this poem. It doesn't begin and doesn't end
in a page, a line or a comma. This full stop is a point

that floats in infinite space just because you distance your gaze from it.
Look, there are clouds on it, orange on the blue evening sky,

sea of sea, sand of sand, and people walking,
sitting, lying, swimming or making love. Choose for yourself

a place and time. Where are you? Now you've found a way
into a point of view. Perhaps you'd like to be born? In this *here,*

now is called by a number: twenty second
of the first, one thousand nine hundred and ninety-five,

twelve thirty, in the afternoon, Sunday. And good that you came.
Tomorrow I'll write the poem you'll live in. Here: this home*

— solely yours. And its location, size, colours and furniture
— your perspective, also its windows, which face

a home or homes on the outskirts of the poem, in its centre or above it:
see its trees pass by, its inhabitants, cafes, and flying saucers,

cavalry, elephants, parchments from which the sea has just withdrawn,
they all flicker between there-is and there-isn't, between a gaze and its focus,

between being and me, between "this" and its names, (me,
me and more me: a pot of cyclamen, a hair

on a bath rail etc.). So go out and see: this poem, given over
to meaningless murmurs, it and I have nothing

but what is between here and I am. (This is not an end-line, here —
I wrote another one.) Now —

* the word "home" or "house" in Hebrew also means "stanza" in a poem

His inside gropes at things, turns outwards

[3]

Come sit down, see: houses return to their places
slowly. The frost lights up the windowpane. One more day.

Come sit down. Coffee or tea? Sugar, milk? That's how it is:
hard boiled egg or sunny side up. Yogurt or sour cream. Jam or honey.

This life, impossible with it
and impossible without: morning or evening, man or woman,

cold or hot — come sit down. What else is new? The sea and the sand
sink into each other, and there's no lifesaver, and no one who interrupts,

and I look at you holding flotsam and jetsam
and there isn't even a ship, and the situation is undefined

and both of us are cut into the same sentence and carry it further,
each for himself. Come sit down,

say: one or many. Slavery or freedom. Me
or you. Love or. How could you know. Fear.

Only in forgetfulness, when we don't have a shore
or footprints, and there's a sound to the words   and there isn't,

and they don't mark the pictures but what gaped
between them and is gone and never existed. Come sit down.

Tomato, cucumber, spring onion, cream cheese,
slices of kummel bread, margarine, salt.

Even if you say: wait, you're dreaming — even if I check
on my place and actions, what will change?

In fact I'm sitting in front of the computer now. In fact
I'm doing all this — from the beginning, everything. In fact

you're sitting in front of a page now, you're hungry to touch the...
as I am. In fact at this very moment you touch

from inside out, devour the world that doesn't stop
spilling out from you: orange on the blue of morning sky, frost

burning on the windowpane, cup of tea — whatever
you chose and came into being. So just this way,

choose now, too: me for example
one breakfast, one more day. Here.

Tendril gropes / coils / on groping tendril

[4]

Already too late to go back and dangerous to stop
what we spoke and so existed, actions like these.

Help yourself. A glass of liqueur, a cigarette, a TV
or any alibi you want (if you don't mind, I'll

continue to write: inside of a thigh, texture of lips, one palm
gathering a handful of a convex reality, a nipple in its middle). True,

this poem repeats what is impossible to repeat
and, as from a door in a desert, it's impossible to leave

without meeting it outside. Look: roads and pavements
air and seaports, communication satellites. Look: outer

space from "here"; in a poem like this that's
a question of relationships like anything else

and not only that, every "there" is already here. Window
gapes towards window   and memories —

devour the whole room: sea shore, palm trees, her boyish body
is stooped over the notebook, her head inclined and her hair, black, smooth, falls

and covers the universe. Lips, inside of a thigh, breasts
that are budding now, a Japanese nose, buttocks.

The one who said and was this order — has no fear, or at least
has forgetfulness, while each moment his gaze buds   on what he sees.

I'll write it now: I'll let it disappear word by word
and not be so much; and each line will begin and end

like a fly landing in a room of mirrors. Once more:
sea of sea, sand of sand. Look and create them,

hold them for a moment between wandering boundaries,
fix them in letters like an orderly cry

to say what there isn't, wasn't, won't be,
and don't bother more than that. Now let go. And again —

When he knows he's crawling, the slough occurs on its own

[5] Hold a world. A cigarette, a glass, lips,
the weight of your limbs on the chair's wooden seat, my face, your face,

autumn leaves on the pavement, a lunch bag, a warm smell
and hands that cover you up before the day's turned off.

Now for a moment: don't hold. Let go. Let them expand
and furnish what's inside you, without being so much of a world,

without placing green on the leaves or
on the remembered palm tree at the sea shore (near

that boyish body, stooping over a notebook).
Let the leaves mingle with the pavement, to rest there,

be not "leaves" at all, not "a cigarette", "a glass",
"lips". Expand in you like excitement,

like sea on a shore. Once they're like this, inside you,
turn them off and on again. Turn off, turn on,

off-on, and again. Now
do the same thing with the world in which you are "you",

a thing among things. Watch it sailing in the expanse
of a body, turn-off-turn-on-turn-off and see

what you're made of. All this is just
the allegory in the story. We'll continue flickering and in a binary rhythm

will continue to say nothing to anyone who asks —
I, you, etc. And, why not, let's make a new allegory:

here, we created this outside world. This orange
on the blue; the "insult", the "hope", what

quivers between us, between there-is and there-isn't, between
this and that. Let's call it.

Hand over hand. (What broke out — touches)

[6]

You say: to be penetrated, to penetrate. Sea-sand, sand-sea
verging on the very centre. Words fall between us

like something broken. Listen, I love you.
But you, having it only your way, exist, exist, exist.

You are not being paid for this and still,
Mr. and Mrs. Other, you stroll along the street as if

you're only a name and have no navel. I
act like you, repeat the movements

which you repeat. Tell me, reflection —
I throw another stone at you — is anyone more actual than me?

I say sand-sea, sea-sand. Like something
broken: a multiplication of faces, legs and hands, like something

that's there. So: enough. Come back to me. I'll let you go
as often as you like.

Now there's no longer a difference between us, except this poem
where some sort of a world lives. Another possibility,

not really different: here, you don't leave at all.
You don't stop coming for a moment. I open

a mirror and turn its pages in front of what's already
written. It's what you are: sadness in front of the blue evening sky,

anger, insult, longing sucking the blue from your chest
or happiness that suddenly spills in front of the blue of that evening sky;

it's a voice which accompanies what, looking,
I see now or don't see. And I see you:

world by world, now by now, one
and yet another one. In this poem that stumbles from page

to page you watch and flicker between letter and letter
and vanish — present in every one of these apparently silent centimetres —

and don't stop coming, and not really coming. So enough, please, don't hide everywhere, talk to me, all of you at once.

What's touching has a face

[7]

Here I sit, on a bench in the park, and bask in the sun.
And next to me, as it's a park, an old lady is sitting. The body

only asks to return to the beginning, to the first performance
that you've already seen over and over in lesser versions.

Then — you remember — the light made us cry, and the world was the centre,
like an underground terminus. Afterwards there were only

faltering explanations, poems maddened by a repetitive yearning,
misunderstood apologies, and letters

that didn't solve a thing. People tired quickly, and rushed to those
who already believed in their existence. Like you and me

they believed in habit without thinking about it, wore it
like a snake's skin every morning. I asked how they were,

shook their hands ("Hello!"), we looked at one another
from above or below   in the same pain. More or less the same thing

was written in books, though in them time was different, full of teeth
biting the back of this time, which in that world wore the world.

There were things without time at all: a checked dress in the wind,
skin under fingers or sunlight, a wound that healed up and disappeared,

purple briarwood buttons, an electric wire
cutting the window in two, the fluttering of a curtain in the morning

or a hiding place among tall grass —
these taught me something everyone knows. You can

simply ignore it, pulling a face: "How are you?",
"Sonofabitch!", "I deem that" etc.; but time exists

by being chased: along an unweeded path the house turns
into a back yard, into balding grass and a bra on a line,

and déjà vu fills up what can be seen with hallucinations
that were earlier called a dream. The way out of the house

passes through scrap-heaps of images of existence, and out of them
the countless arms of those begging for faces stretch

toward you with a thinning howl: see me, see me and believe in me,
I'm your son that you loved, take me to you, take —

and be redeemed. I cry with them out of stupidity, cry
and don't look back, don't look back. At night

they greet your other faces: hungrier. You shut
the dictionary in which "life" is only plural,* open a book,

a fridge, a bottle, a T.V. But despite everything
they're here — they come out of the freezer like a genie from a bottle

and hop into the screen. You shut your eyes and let go. Let them do to you.
And already the stage lights up, a curtain rising fold by fold (or rather

veil after veil), a forest of eyes, sounds and your-body in front of you
appears from nowhere, rolls out from inside the stomach leaving you no *I*

beyond itself. You go down stone stairs to the river,
strip naked, still dancing. Two brownish youths

splash water on a buffalo   until it gives in and goes under. A hawk dives
into a reflection of a banyan tree, inside the net laid, it seems,

by a fisherman; outside   the alarm of a parked car goes up and down.
You extricate yourself from the blanket; still full of eyes, you gather your body

and drag your feet to the shower like a recurring dream. Good morning,
I say, and take you out slowly slowly

from the mirror to the towel, that brings you back further
into this body, and dresses you with a face. You

begin to use a palate, a tongue, a throat, lips, and extricate from there
a hoarse sound that tests the air: "I —"

*the word "life" in Hebrew is plural, "life" and "lives" are distinguished only by context.

A face weaned from being a mouth

[8]

What have I to do with this poem: now, when my gaze lingers
one more moment after or between the words, when they haven't

yet separated from the world and only desire stands
between the beginning and the end, between what's inside

and what isn't? Since this poem has no subject, just like
you or me,

since this poem has no subject, but only a predicate,
and all the rest is still no more present

than the blotch of light after you look at the sun. Only movement
is the subject here; the poem rests upon it. And all the other things

are drawn, it seems, from impressions of space; indicated, it appears,
by the flight of movement: from here it's a tree, from here onwards

the scent of a tree, from here   the roots stop being earth. Up to here
a leaf (a divided green surface, its margins dented, flawed

by a brown stain or two); now another line — it's the petiole —
and soon: a branch. Inside there's water, and outside there's water

whose names are "lake" or "rain". Outside there's light, it's called "day";
inside it's something else, which concerns photosynthesis, and behind —

"shadow". And this is wonderful, because one can say, "Here is an oak",
"Here is my neighbour, Michelle", and even more:

"Hi, I missed you", "Go to hell!", "Where
were you all this time?"; but a tree doesn't

grow or wither   except the way the world does:
it's even registered as "tree" in the world inventory.

So let's keep distance as distance: the hand that's between you and me
is the memory and the forgetfulness   of the One who has no outside.

The mouth that suckled is the mouth that nurses with a howl

[9]

No matter where you look it's here. "This poem" is returning home
from everywhere to everywhere, and no-where's free of it —

crossing landmasses by way of stormy water, climbing air into a never-ending sky,
forgetting how your face looks, till suddenly it emerges like memory

from what's seen. You sit inside, early early in the morning,
and can't help seeing:

out of the fog, a fig tree grows in the old cistern
and the grass is tall and moist, still delineated, still green to the touch.

And yet, what could I say to a tree   when its bark touches my cheek
and it has no visible beginning? All this conversation

is a single word without names, faded, continuous, remaining:
where do you end and where, renewing again and again,

do you begin? Where does it happen, where did it happen
and why does it hurt, and what is it that hurts, and what,

after all, brought us back our faces?
Sheep ripped and chewed above the cistern. Light examined palms of leaves. Time

was far off again. And again, "This poem . . ." Nothing,
nothing.

In water he is a sea anemone. A carnivore extending the arms of a flower

[10]

And yet here we are, equipped with everything. Feet,
back, biceps, eye, ear, nose, tongue and skin. We're here:

faces and interiors, neighbours, cities and nations. We're here,
breathing, living. And what does one learn from this?

Some say life *is* continuing in the face of the alternative;
some say — conquest; some stretch an equals sign

between life and its absence; and some say that life
was given us to serve those   whose lives

are not a life. I say: you.
And this is easily explained: once again night envelops

what can be seen. At home lamps are lit. And in the light there's no glance
except the one from the mirror, nothing except what sees me

seeing it; and it brings not release but longing, not death
but life. And I remove my gaze from the warm and the cold — night envelops everything —

and I long for the one who sees me through touching,
and I don't remember a thing. Only this.

On the abrasive, glassy sand, he understands

[11]
Snake, you say. I say serpent.
And then you say that snakes were always also a symbol for medicine,

wisdom, and longevity. Snake and not serpent, you and not a biting reptile,
fly above the main street, land gracefully on a cherry tree

and sing and sing, like a nightingale to its mate, beautiful from so much self:
the phone bursts out like howls at the end of an alley

the fax throws up other people's souls
the computer is in SAVE and there's no lifesaver:

it begins again, only begins.
It already was.

This is not the poem that is *the poem*, as this is the poem that's not dedicated to you;
I rest this poem on any face I choose,

I'm not waiting for a reply, not waiting for you to be
in front of my pointing finger in "reality" — Hello to you, reality! —

that's like a girl mounting any imagination   like a rider on a horse
galloping on the "merely-image" which no place is free of

and no matter where one gallops it comes and comes with one.
It's clear enough when one's wandering from awareness of this

to awareness of that, and a little less clear
when we agree so much   about images that are here between us

and images-that-are-there. Say, is "awakening"
one thing? (Is falling arriving?) This poem,

like the world, like a recurring dream, isn't coming and won't arrive
at "world" from dream, day from night,

nor the other way around. The poem says its place is "twilight",
and it's already inside it, without needing

either sun or sunset. A picture of consciousness emerges
like a nestling from an egg of warm possibility: *there* is what thrills

and so exists; the picture of consciousness hatches, this is how what-is exists.
I'm only describing what I saw or heard —

picture by picture, as if there's a line-up for being; white stains
of a flock of seagulls on the sea, sand dunes

grooved by water which toppled from above.
And this is a daily act, of which forks and what they impale

are made, and I am too. Say, and I'll be.
Going around the room without seeing, without remembering a thing,

and looking for an ashtray. All this is written. Now you. What's the difference now
between the poem and you?

He's coming

[12]

Will you come? Will I be happy to meet you? Will the door
be the gate? Will three fires still greet your face

and will their names still be explicit? Heart-fire,
head-fire, fire between-the-legs. Is your face

firewood to their flames now, is your face
immortal as they are? Will these "eternal fires" stay alight?

Aren't butterflies consumed? Do fires burn like this,
like breath, like the stomach fire

that consumes bread? Will I see you when you sit in front of me?
My beloved, my lover, my question mark! From horizon to horizon

an over-there occupies my stomach. Where does this path start
that has no direction? Where does this string end

which is all end? And who goes that way, even when I don't?
Except for two arches and a dent between them, except for a slope

into a collarbone, what kind of sign is this
that breaks from the chest a long call: "Come!" — "Don't come!" ?

And another line goes up from the poem to touch the image, but
you aren't there either. We don't know each other. For now

we don't have contempt for happiness. And what's happiness? A calm sacrificial fire
on which our faces are laid, and warmth that brims over

from the cavities of our stomach, our chest. For now you only remember
that "outside the darkness is freezing". But afterwards —

it's hot. Smoke rises and something burns, and if we continue — we'll be consumed.
Instead of this, at a distance, we sweat

and not from excitement. We wave a newspaper, a letter,
create a breeze and open a window to inhale

the cold night air. And it's already late. Someone
has to return home, and behind "Come!", "Don't come!", again,

we understand: come whenever you don't come. Tomorrow it'll be possible
to see pain in the sand where returning footprints were printed.

Instead of all this I shut the door and open the wall,
and on my door I write: Don't come from here, always come from there.

Far from himself, he sees his self

[13]   And when you come, remember this, remember how we got here:
       live Alpha-Betas remained miles behind

       on a slalom track of here and gone, flickered for another
       moment, vanished from the mirror. What the Alfa-Romeo had to say

       was swallowed before we heard it: only this ability, to shatter,
       kept us from falling upwards, apart; after it

       a sky's thud. We were riding time; could have overtaken
       a thousand more crashes, waited for the flickering blue to approach from behind,

       getting out that moment before the licence is asked for: What did you want?
       What did you intend? What were you thinking? You could have got killed.

       This can also be asked about a woman or a poem
       or a look. But nothing will satisfy,

       nothing, other than complete exteriority, if there's such a thing.
       And what's so alluring about this *there*, if not the *here*

54

that's been placed in such doubt that it exists more than ever —
and still not enough. When you come here remember this,

sit in front of me and fall straight into your own eyes; and fall deep,
far, so there's room

for me to fall too. It's always possible to stop at the side of the road:
words, excuses, plugs, gasket —

to call this "misunderstanding" — and blink beside the carriage-way
at any blotch   seen out the corner of the eye: take me.

A seed sown in sand waits.

[14]   It's very easy to betray me with me. Try, I'll even forgive it.
— You don't. Now it's necessary to court you for hours,

to leave flowers on the desk, notes
on the dining table, to invite you for a fish supper,

to water you with gin and tonic (long).
You walk around for days with wide eyes

or play with a ball or a teddy-bear as if they're the only things
in the world. All this as the newspapers are full of horrible

reports. Someone shot himself in the head on a live broadcast
and the same thing also happened last week on *Dynasty*.

The memory works like a tired fisherman; crocodiles, sharks
and even sardines fight over the bait

as over the boards of a sinking ship. All this
while you sit in the living-room: what are you afraid of? I give you my hand

and take you to the sea. The sea's stormy, just like
twenty eight years ago when a stray shark bit

a woman smelling of blood here. You return
to your teddy-bear-and-ball, and don't stop not-looking at the sea.

I take out a pencil and paper and draw you a poem:
the sea's stormy, your feet sink enveloped

in wet sand, the smell of seaweed and salt, and miles of blue
broken white strips. Now you remember,

even though it never happened like this. You lift your gaze
and remember everything.

More —

[15]

So I don't even look at you but prefer the window.
And the eye, dappled black and grey, is zooming in

to discover the broken outlines of a growth
whose heart is one and invisible.

Like an elephant's dry skin, grooved with islands, ancient,
the olive tree gathers its folds

into a concavity of old shadow-sunken curves, returns
to stretch in ridges roughened by the sun's touches. There

above a hump of peel a baby leans toward a breast —
a rusty nail.

Beyond this I don't look, don't think. How can I
think about leaves turning silver outside in the twilight,

about the sky above them, above my gaze?
How can I think about infinity and the void now, when you

are about to die? And as you are about to die, how can I not think about you? How?
Think perhaps about loved ones

who haven't yet been, maybe even about those who are alive?
Think that even in this there's still a thought about you,

and even believe it? Can I be that strong
only because of what you've done to me now? Because you're dead? Tomorrow

I'll write you a few words, an epitaph or at least a note —
something poetic, for example, "Here lies a dancer".

And if this isn't enough to bury you, I'll elaborate for sure:
"Water me", I'll write on the marble. "Water me,

I am thirsty. Water me and not with water. Water me,
and not with clear logic. Water me, and not with a name.

Water me and not with wine. Water me and nothing else,
water me. Beauty won't do, love won't do, God won't do —

even this life won't do, nor any life. Water me,
I am thirsty".

Drowning, he breathes living water

[16]

My Narcissus, in the end you got used to it. You sprouted gills
on the sides of your neck and sliding down down

sprawled among stems and water. And the echo became a wave
and the reflection a place and you looked and looked and looked

toward the skyline of water. And leapt
out again   to me.

And the thunder returned to silence, the water to being a screen,
the eye — to marble. You came back into me.

And the echo became a voice and the reflection a face
and you were released.

Come
sit down.

He remembers. Outside is torn inward from him

No longer clear   how to fold all of this poem back.
The poem is a memory: like a sun

that stayed in the eye after a glance at the sun, so
this poem, line after line. A man

climbs the stairs again to his second floor apartment.
This man, a hook for another line, opens the door

and gropes for the electric switch. Afterwards to the fridge.
Opens the bottle and doesn't make an allegory out of it.

You say there are facts   and all this didn't happen in the poem
but on the stairs and in the apartment on Sunday at nine,

and he was you, and anyway you returned
to feed the cat. The poem, you say, is like

a sun that stayed in the eye after a glance at the eye
that glanced at the sun. I say the poem's no further away

than the knowledge that "Here is a cat", "Here are words". Here
too are worlds of memories   to be remembered from now on.

True, I forgot to talk about the cat; it never
existed in the poem. OK, so the cat gorged from a dustbin

all afternoon, then displayed an appetite   only out of compassion
for the loneliness of such a man. Yet, after all,

in this poem no cat will remain indifferent
to the smell of chicken leftovers — or fail to detect them among its lines —

despite their being well sealed in a plastic doggy-bag
in the neighbourhood restaurant just before closing time.

Even in its fullness, a tree is nothing but a seed

[18]   By now, perhaps, we could already read the poem
without opening the book. Now, once all this is over,

it won't perish even after its end, even if it's to be
an undeciphered script on a monument   that once an aeon carbon dioxide winds

reveal on the face of Mars.
That's it no further away than this line, and all I can see here

is only what you see: stains, pictures,
faces of here-is; and the further you go, the closer you come.

Picture by picture, time spreads over the whole land, but still
the noon seagulls   stretch their necks once more into a night

filled with dreams of fish. Everything is drawn on the sand with a confident hand:
this poem was the poem of another century, not different from the one

seen in memory. Like a bottle from a ship, like a demon from a bottle,
among the grains accumulated on the sandglass shore, this poem

will be seen in public entirely by chance.   Will simultaneously
run naked on two shores, fall shamelessly in love

with every niche and heap, un-annotated curse
its comic blessings, and while listening: will listen.

And without knowing what's possible, what isn't possible, and what's not what,
will only render one plus one, one minus one, and get

the one by one and two by two of if-not-"I" — then who?
And then you'll return home, open the door, and grope

for the electric switch. Afterwards to the fridge, open the bottle —
and you won't make an allegory out of this, not even an example.

Just shut the mirror, look at the lamp, and warm like a butterfly
in another mirror in which there's no face, where you see

only sea of sea, sand of sand, orange on the blue of evening sky;
in which you hear : "Come, sit down."

And when you see and hear, you'll be glad to live in this poem,
to look with me at the hair on the bath rail, a pot of cyclamen

or any other being that passed by here; and your gaze will land
like a naked "I" inside this flowerpot-ness,

cool, full of the weight of moist earth on your walls and base
and your weight leaning on the floor. Or the old woman on the park bench —

alongside the rustling of trees, children's voices and mothers' small-talk,
warmth permeates your shrivelling limbs and, half-asleep,

awakens them to remember without words
a touch, another bench, another moment of —. Thoughts

pass through you like clouds in a sky of no-thing, their destination
is unknown and they have no tomorrow. The wind plays with your hair

as with leaves, children's voices and mothers' small-talk,
like background music. And the world is large, back and forth

it's full of your eyes. Stone stair, a hawk falling
into the reflection of a banyan tree inside a net laid,

apparently, by a fisherman. And again   you place a bare footstep
or again gather your wings, let your body fall

through the air. Or only the surface of water,
capering with branches and greenery: you are a living mirror, a world —

bodiless, enfolding into you another hawk, another tree — and you sway
with the river. And finally, while your skin, burnt by the sun,

is cooling in water up to your chest, you pull and pull
the net to you, your muscles stretch to the weight, and the gaze

through the slits of your eyes observes flexible silvery backs
and quivers with them between crisscrossed strings.

And then you'll say: this poem does exist. This poem —
its trees, its inhabitants, cafes and flying saucers,

cavalry, elephants, parchments, that your gaze withdrew from
just now — this poem is solely yours, and is opened

by the way you look at it. Here, look at me; see, inside me, that which sees;
here, you wrote another line.

Afterword:
***Poem* and the Sacrifice of Being**

The title of this book sounds a challenge. It is as if there can be no poem beyond the world of *Poem*; as if this is a text which takes itself to the limits of what a poem can be. Or as if this poem, in making itself, creates a world of experience so alive that it in the same movement dispenses with questions of literary identity. In that case *Poem* is an *un title*; like an *Untitled* painting it forces the viewer to read the thing itself. A self-transcending note, it reminds us that the work of a poem may be experiential rather than linguistic. And yet language is still part of that experience:

> And these words   their taste is full of the taste of
>
> being, of a tone that accompanies the sight with wonder
> and not with a thought-slamming din. And this is the poem.

Language moves in and out of the experience which is human *being*; coloured by that experience and colouring it. We do not experience only through language — *Poem* says "I long for the one who sees me through touching" — nor does language come up to the edges of experience. Amir Or is no Aristotelean who believes that language, in chopping up the world into names, presents its true nature to the naturally corresponding human mind. He is a poet whose origins are in the radical uncertainties of the twentieth century, which trumped the death of God with the death of the Human. Or at least of

74

humanism, of the comforting belief that human nature might be the repository of some ultimate dignifying dimension of meaning. Perhaps this public execution of the human is seen in the scale of contemporary public planning, trade, discourse, violence. This is an order of things which *Poem* resists. The turn it makes repeatedly is towards the locus of meaning, towards the intimate register of experience as it is had.

Why is this turn repeated? Isn't it enough to present an idea, perhaps to illustrate it? But *Poem* is a sustained work of experience: it is a self-resisting work. Amir Or, like Nietzsche and Heidegger — the great philosophers of the nature of language — knows that language finally speaks only itself: that in order to meet our experience in and through language we must constantly resist, not its grammar or capacities, but the closure of its logic. Once narrative is locked into language, it becomes a told thing, not something happening: once an experience is caught by language we have the words instead of the experience itself.

Or manages to resist *Poem*'s desire to complete itself by constantly shifting positions. We have the filmic clarity of a moment at the beach, a breakfast table in Tel Aviv. There are tableaux — an encounter with the mythic self in the fancy dress of Narcissus, a Lilliputian thought-world — and the realities of the world of the senses. Or unlocks the conventional register of the seen with taste, touch and, in this open-mouthed poem, the orality of the text. Sometimes the narrator explains, sometimes he leads the reader through their own experience, sometimes he brings that reader into his: we see a lover through his eyes, we experience his memory, desire, even his difficulty in waking up. The effect is of the collisions and colliding consciousnesses of life itself. A calling-together of the nature of things.

What is that nature? Or's poetry does not name the stable boundaries of things — a clockwork world kept alive in the metaphysics of universalised "knowledge" — but it is not a metaphysical desert either. As his narrative titles — or are they epigraphs? — show, *Poem* does not differentiate between being and meaningful experience. To find meaning is to be(come) alive:

Water me,

I am thirsty. Water me and not with water. Water me,
and not with clear logic. Water me, and not with a name.

Water me and not with wine. Water me and nothing else,
water me. Beauty won't do, love won't do, God won't do —

even this life won't do, nor any life. Water me,
I am thirsty.

The intimately-specific, unassuageable Everyman who offers this as an epitaph — who sheds possible metaphysics, identities, ways of thinking like a seed-pod or a carapace as he goes — is also a lover. *Poem* is also a love poem: to world, to experience, to the reader, to language and poetry. Sometimes the woman who figures as lover is addressed; sometimes that "you" reaches out of the poem to include the reader; sometimes "you" is also the narrator whose consciousness we have entered, "since this poem has no subject, just like you or me". Fleeting and ambiguous as a love-affair, these shifts of position sometimes suggest ambivalence — *Poem* is no praise-poem — and sometimes the unimportance of boundaries. Earth, root, tree and leaf are in a relation not of difference but of continuity with each other: and with the experience of which they form part. It is not identity but presence which patterns being.

The other we live in relation to — whether human or environmental — has always formed an "ethical" part of the meaning we try to find in experience. This poem of radical self-exploration is also a radical refusal of solipsism. Language is:

> wonderful, because then one can say, "Here is an oak",
> "Here is my neighbour, Michelle", and even more:
>
> "Hi, I missed you", "Go to hell!", "Where
> were you all this time?".

Poem transcends the political, yet is immediate and contemporary; it is local, personal, yet eschews the tradition of the exceptional individual; it demands that the mundane be understood in all its profundity; in resisting poetic traditions it shows us what poetry can be. It is difficult, paradoxical and beautiful. Constantly breaking itself down in order to create itself, *Poem* demonstrates that to keep making a world of meaning, to keep "adding another line" — that most private task — requires us to sacrifice ourselves into the fullest possible openness.

Fiona Sampson

Part of The **Waxwing Poetry Project** is the hope of getting people involved in thinking how the world may abolish war as a legitimate means of resolving political conflict between states. What is vital is the development of alternatives in protecting the innocent, restraining aggressors and overcoming injustice. Nothing new in this dream, perhaps, yet any dream may one day become reality? Attempts at justifying war have always been intellectually and spiritually vulnerable as well as practically inadequate. It is very doubtful if any actual war fulfilled the traditional criteria of *jus ad bellum* and *jus in bello*. In our own time it has become impossible to see how criteria such as having exhausted all non-violent means ("last resort"), non-combatant immunity and proportionality can ever be observed. "Just war theory" can no longer be maintained. It is time that all concerned people be drawn into an examination and development of alternatives to war. The illusion is hot held that the call for the abolition of war will bring an immediate or even quick end to the massacres called war. Interrogation and dialogue are hoped for. However, it was once assumed that slavery was simply part of "the natural order". Those calling for slavery's abolition were thought to be foolish utopian dreamers. Slavery, of course, still exists in multiple guises but no one thinks aloud that slavery can be justified or that a public profit can be made from it. Let the twenty-first century be for war what the nineteenth was for slavery : the era of its abolition.